3rd Edition

Upper Intermediate

MARKET LEADER

Business English Test File

Lewis Lansford

PEARSON
Longman

FINANCIAL
TIMES

Contents

The recordings for the listening sections of these tests are on a separate *Test Master* CD-ROM, which is free with the *Market Leader Third Edition Upper Intermediate Teacher's Resource Book*. They are also on the *Market Leader* website at *www.market-leader.net*.

Entry test

🔊 2 **Listen to a conversation between Isobel Reed, an HR manager, and her assistant Joyce Payne. Look at her current diary page below and then answer the questions about her new schedule. You will hear the conversation twice.**

Mon	Tue	Wed	Thu	Fri
17	**18**	**19**	**20**	**21**
08:00 Directors' meeting	*10:00 Meet with Production – discuss recruitment policy*	*12:30 Lunch with Stephanie Banks* *15:30 Meet with Pietro and Irena – finalise monthly report*	*09:00 Departmental meeting* *15:00 Meet with legal team – go through employment contracts*	*10:00 Briefing for new management trainees*

1   Where will Isobel travel to this week?

2   Which days will she be away?

3   What day and time does Isobel want to reschedule the departmental meeting to?

4   What else does Isobel ask Joyce to check about this meeting?

5   What is the new deadline for the monthly report?

6   What day and time does Isobel suggest holding the meeting with Joyce and Terry?

   Day:

   Time:

7   What other rearrangement must be dealt with urgently?

8   When should Joyce tell the trainees about the changes?

9   How is the meeting with the legal team being changed?

10 When will Isobel be available to discuss other changes?

LANGUAGE **A** Complete the text with the most appropriate word(s).

Trendspotter: Capsule hotels

Hotels usually try to offer their guests comfort on their travels. But when Sir Stelios Haji-Ioannou, the Easyjet founder, ...[11] (opens / opened) his first Easyhotel, the idea was to give overnighters a no-frills room that ....[12] (is exchanging / exchanged) space and luxury for lower prices. Since then, the capsule hotel ....[13] (has taken / took) off and sacrificing space no longer means giving up luxury.

In New York's West Village, The Jane ....[14] (offers / offer) rooms of about five square metres, each with a television, DVD player, Ipod dock and free WiFi. For more luxury, the rooms at The Pod Hotel in Midtown ....[15] (placed / place) more emphasis on interior decor, and also have music streaming in the bathrooms.

Accommodation that is similar to a ship's basic bed ....[16] (is / are) increasingly popular at airports. Simon Woodroffe, creator of the Yo! Sushi restaurant chain, ...[17] (have / has) Yotels at Gatwick and Heathrow in London, and Amsterdam Schiphol. Rooms ....[18] (have / have been) flat-screen TVs and wireless Internet. Operating on a similar model, Arch Group designers Alex Goryainov and Mikhail Krymov ....[19] (have developed / develop) the sleek, minimalist Sleepbox, around 60 of which are ....[20] (being / been) installed in Dubai airport.

FINANCIAL TIMES

B Match the questions and statements (21–25) to the responses (a–e).

21 What do you think of the new flex-time system? ....

22 I'd like to know why I haven't received my refund yet. ....

23 We really need delivery by the 30th. ....

24 Can I interrupt you for a moment?
I need to ask about sales forecasts. ....

25 I'm really sorry I'm late. My car broke down. ....

a) I'll look into it right away.

b) I'd like to finish, if I may.

c) That's all right. We've just started.

d) If you order now, that won't be a problem.

e) I think it's working really well.

VOCABULARY

A Choose the verb that cannot be used with each noun.

26 relocate / grow / run / open   an office

27 resign / fire / recruit / employ   workers

28 break into / dominate / decline / enter   a market

29 charge / make / raise / boost   money

30 increase / cut / remain / discount   prices

B Complete the sentences with the words in the box.

> company   copy   details   distribution   document   effect
> journey   products   region   yourselves

To:	Simon Wade (Simon.Wade@computadist.com)
From:	Hidekazu Tanaka
Subject:	Distribution agreement

Dear Mr Wade

It was very good to see you again at our meeting in Osaka last month.
I hope you had a safe .... ³¹ home afterwards.

We agreed that your .... ³² will take over the
.... ³³ of our .... ³⁴ in North America for three
years, with .... ³⁵ from September 1.

Full .... ³⁶ of the agreement are included in the attached
.... ³⁷. Can you please check this and, if all is in order,
sign and return one .... ³⁸ to me.

We look forward to continuing to develop our business in the
.... ³⁹ in association with .... ⁴⁰.

Best wishes

Hidekazu Tanaka

A **Read the first half of the article (to line 49) and decide if these statements are true (t) or false (f).**

41 All of the companies making the changes are car makers.

42 There was a problem with some of Toyota's cars in the US.

43 Chinese workers have recently gone on strike.

44 Komatsu plans to bring Chinese managers to manage plants in Japan.

45 None of Komatsu's Chinese subsidiaries are run by Chinese mangers.

B **Read the second half of the article. Match the company or person (46–50) with the description (a–e).**

46 Shiseido ....   a) will soon have overseas top management in about 16 of its foreign subsidiaries.

47 Kao ....   b) plans to assess Japanese and overseas managers in the same way.

48 Toyota ....   c) will train Japanese and overseas managers similarly.

49 Didier Leroy ....   d) will become head of a Toyota plant in Texas.

50 An American ....   e) is going to run Toyota's European sales and manufacturing.

Japanese groups seek local leaders abroad

A number of Japanese manufacturers on Tuesday said they were planning to promote more foreign executives to top positions at their overseas operations, opening the way for potentially significant cultural changes as the focus of their businesses shifts abroad.

Moves to localise management by companies as diverse as Toyota, construction-equipment maker Komatsu and Itochu, the trading house, follow a series of problems at some Japanese companies' foreign operations that some have blamed on a shortage of managers with deep local ties.

The problems have included recent strikes at Japanese autoparts makers in China and the recall by Toyota beginning late last year of millions of vehicles, a majority of them in the US. Over the past month, eight Honda and Toyota suppliers in China have been hit by strikes, which in many cases have forced the shutdown of the larger assembly plants that rely on their output.

Komatsu, which makes heavy equipment for the building and mining industries, on Tuesday said it planned to install Chinese managers as the top executives of all 16 of its subsidiaries in China in the next two years.

The company said that none of its operations in China had been affected by the recent spate of strikes, but it acknowledged that it had faced 'contentious labour issues' in the past. Only one of the subsidiaries is currently run by a Chinese national. Itochu, which trades food, clothing and industrial raw materials through a network of about 140 offices and affiliates round the world, said it was looking to increase the proportion of non-Japanese senior managers outside Japan to half from the current level of about 30 per cent.

"We are moving forward with a truly global human resources strategy" the company said.

Japanese companies are hardly alone in sending expatriate managers to run operations overseas. But the relative homogeneity of their domestic recruiting pool, combined with a reluctance to hire mid-career executives from other companies, has left Japanese groups with a less diverse roster of global managers than many of their US or European rivals. Other Japanese companies looking to strengthen their foreign management include the cosmetics makers Shiseido and Kao. Shiseido said it was scrapping separate performance-review systems for Japanese and overseas managers in place of a unified standard. Kao said it was integrating management training for all its employees regardless of nationality.

Last week, Toyota shifted more responsibility to its non-Japanese managers in the US and Europe, promoting a group of local executives to run factories and other operations outside Japan. Once the changes take effect on July 1, a third of its 48 foreign subsidiaries will be run by non-Japanese.

Among them, Didier Leroy, a Frenchman, is to become the first non-Japanese to head Toyota's sales and manufacturing businesses in Europe. Two Americans will meanwhile replace Japanese managers as heads of major assembly plants in Texas and Indiana.

WRITING

Alex James, a business associate from the US, will be visiting your office next week. You have not met before. He has just sent you an e-mail to let you know he will be arriving at 9 p.m. on Monday. Write a polite, friendly e-mail of 100–150 words to him.

Include the following points:

- company driver will meet Alex James at the airport (carrying a sign with his name)
- room booked at Metro Hotel – hotel normally used by your company
- informed hotel about late arrival
- hotel: small, comfortable, quiet (see website: www.citymetrotel.com)
- on Tuesday you will meet him 8:45 a.m. at hotel and walk to office (10 minutes)
- wish him pleasant trip

SPEAKING

You are going to have a speaking test that will last 10–15 minutes. The examiner will ask you to spend five minutes preparing the short presentation below. Make notes if you wish.

A group of eight British people has just arrived in your country and will be working at your company or college for the next six months. Make an informal presentation of about five minutes and include the following:

- a friendly welcome to the group.
- any daily routines they will need to be aware of (starting and finishing times, lunch, meetings, etc.).
- any aspects of culture that may be different in your country and the US.

Progress test 1 (Units 1–3)

A 🔊 3 **Listen to a phone call between Darren Larson and his manager, Liz Parks. Choose the best answer, a, b, or c to complete the sentences.**

1 Business in Vietnam is .... each quarter.

   a) improving   b) getting worse   c) about the same

2 Sales in Thailand have .... recently .

   a) increased   b) decreased   c) not changed

3 Darren says the agent in Thailand has been ....

   a) promoted   b) replaced   c) transferred

4 The new agent ....

   a) has already started   b) will start next month   c) has not been chosen

5 Liz .... the sales conference in Singapore.

   a) has already attended   b) won't attend   c) plans to attend

B **Listen again. For each function (6–10), tick the correct person.**

		Darren	Liz
6	asks for repetition	[ ]	[ ]
7	asks for clarification	[ ]	[ ]
8	has problems with understanding	[ ]	[ ]
9	asks for further information	[ ]	[ ]
10	complains of technical problems	[ ]	[ ]

A **Complete the sentences with the words in the box.**

bush   grapevine   nutshell   stick   wall

11 I heard it on the .... you've been promoted.

12 I asked Rudy to say yes or no, but he just beat around the ....

13 Look, in a .... , my trip to Singapore was a huge success.

14 I think you got the wrong end of the .... I'm not going on holiday, I'm going on a business trip.

15 John just doesn't listen. It's like talking to a brick ....

B Complete the multi-word verbs with *off*, *on* or *up*.

Lufthansa pilots cancel strike

Lufthansa pilots have called ....¹⁶ strike action planned for next week after new talks were set ....¹⁷ with the German airline.

The announcement late on Wednesday averted, or at least put ....¹⁸, a four-day stoppage that could have cost

¹⁰ Lufthansa tens of millions of euros.

The union's action had built .... ¹⁹ the dispute into one of the worst to hit Germany in recent years, adding to a wave of ¹⁵ industrial action across the European airline sector, which has also affected British Airways.

In the end, the stoppage ended after

24 hours when the two sides agreed to ²⁰ carry ....²⁰ negotiating. Lufthansa says strike action costs it at least €25m a day.

C Choose the correct word to complete each sentence.

21 We're meeting tomorrow to discuss the new (market / marketing) strategy.

22 Can we discuss the (sales / price) figures? I was expecting an increase, not a decrease.

23 We're excited about the launch of the new (product / brand) range in South America.

24 I'd like you to meet Liam. He's the one who organised the successful advertising (image / campaign) in London last year.

25 We have brand (loyalty / leader), we just need to increase our market share.

VOCABULARY

A Complete the e-mail with the words in the box.

articulate customer focus identity market marketing misjudged product sensitive underperformed

To: Kate.Richardson@marketresearchers.com

From: Gill.Morton@gpgroup.com

Subject: Market research

Dear Kate

You may remember we met at the Memphis Technology Trade Show last spring. I was very impressed with your presentation on your company's successful ....²⁶ strategy for one of your clients in Australia.

I'm visiting Philadelphia next week, and I'd like to meet with you if you'll be around. We're preparing for a ....²⁷ launch in a developing ....²⁸, and I think your firm would be in a good position to help us develop our brand ....²⁹.

Our last big product ....³⁰ in this same market, partly because we ....³¹ the loyalty of the competition's ....³² base. We don't want to repeat that failure, so we're looking for someone who can run ....³³ groups and be ....³⁴ to market feedback. This person also needs to be ....³⁵ enough to communicate a clear brief to the advertising agency.

Let me know if you have time to meet next week.

Best wishes

Gill

SKILLS   **A**   **Choose the appropriate phrase (a–h) to complete these conversations.**

a)   we met somewhere

b)   went to Carmen Diaz's presentation

c)   was given your name

d)   in sales or product development

e)   see we're in the same line of work

f)   could try Pietro Sylvani

g)   we met some time ago

h)   mentioned your name

A: Hello. You don't know me, but I'm Jeff Watson. I 36
by Janice Hayes – we used to work together in Personnel at Rank Xerox.

B: Oh, yes.

A: I'm looking for someone to help out with some training and Janice .... 37.

B: I see.

A: Haven't .... 38 before?

B: Yes, I think .... 39. Was it at the supply chain conference in Miami?

A: Yes, that's right. We both .... 40.

A: I need to find someone who can help with our distribution in Italy.

B: You .... 41.

A: Isn't he in Shanghai?

B: No, he's back in Rome now.

A: Hi. My name's Roger Lee.

B: Hi, Roger. I'm Erki Jenssen. I .... 42.

A: Yes, that's right. Are you .... 43 ?

B   **Put the words in the correct order to make sentences.**

44   morning strategy marketing purpose our of discuss the to meeting is this

The ....

45   I've idea heard a best long the time for

That's ....

46   they however are crazy want you all your ideas, think

We ....

47   other about ideas this we do can about what ?

Any ....

48   New York City was thinking we maybe go should to

I ....

49   Manhattan hotel in could go just four-star for a

We ....

50   will a idea, that's, money good because save it

Yes, ...

A **Read the article and decide if these statements are true (t) or false (f).**

51 Very few Facebook users log in every day.

52 Business schools understand the value of social and business networking.

53 Most business schools are very happy for their students to use Facebook.

54 Universities' intranets are usually very similar in look and feel to Facebook.

55 BusinessBecause.com is a social networking site aimed at business schools.

56 BusinessBecause.com is specialised for business schools, but reaches a global market.

57 BusinessBecause.com has been in business since 2004.

58 Haas School of Business uses Facebook alongside its own network.

Social networking: Schools struggle to balance openness with control

It is ancient history in Internet terms, but when Facebook was launched in 2004, only college students could join. It opened up to everybody in 2006, and now has more than 400m users, half of whom log in daily.

So along with the world's biggest brands and celebrities, it is no surprise to find that business schools are joining the rush into social media. Universities can use such networks to keep in touch with their alumni, fundraise, attract students or even help them find jobs.

However, for most business schools, the rise of Facebook and its more corporate-minded cousin, LinkedIn, also presents a dilemma. Many have already invested in an internal network for keeping in touch with students and sharing course notes securely. But college IT budgets can't match the resources available to a company dedicated to building such sites and clunky software means many students prefer Facebook to the official intranet.

"It's a very difficult decision." says Soumitra Dutta, a co-author of *Throwing Sheep in the Boardroom*, a corporate guide to social networking. "The natural tendency for most universities is control – they want to own the network. But the public networks are very popular and have much better functionality. Most schools are still struggling with this decision."

Trying to bridge the gap between public and specialist networks is BusinessBecause.com, a news and social media site for business schools, that recently launched from the UK.

"Schools are good at communicating with their own alumni and students but it's tough for students to connect with their counterparts at other schools – in the same city, let alone on the other side of the world" says co-founder Kate Jillings. "Networks such as Facebook and LinkedIn are too big. Schools and students need to be able to search for what they want easily and feel comfortable about being open within a specialist community."

Less than a year old, Business-Because is already being used by Cass Business School in London and the George Washington School of Business in Washington DC. But Ms Jillings says not every university has responded so well. "Considering that these schools are supposed to be at the forefront of business innovation, it's been hard to convince some of their marketing departments of the merits of social media."

Being close to Silicon Valley, that was not so much of a problem for the Haas School of Business at Berkeley. It has created a Facebook fan page to bring together automatically the various Haas groups that are spread across the network. That page now has more than 4,750 fans – out of a total of 30,000 alumni, although that ratio is improving as Facebook attracts more over-35s.

Haas also creates a private Facebook group for MBA students to meet each other virtually before they arrive in California, which is especially useful for international students. The school also operates a private, internal network with 8,000 members.

It seems sociable students and networking alumni will have to remember several logins for some time yet. But whether public or private, using at least one of these sites is 'crucial' for today's MBAs, says Prof Dutta. "They want to keep in contact with their peer group and what better way is there to do it?"

B **Choose the best word or phrase to complete each sentence.**

59 When it launched, Facebook was .... to students.

    a) closed   **b)** only available   **c)** marketed mostly

60 Universities .... social media networks.

    a) use   **b)** fail to understand   **c)** discourage the use of

61 Many business schools have their own intranet that they feel ....
Facebook.

    a) is much better than   **b)** could be replaced with   **c)** competes with

62 The article says that business schools don't have the .... resources
available to big companies such as Facebook.

    a) financial   **b)** IT   **c)** networking

63 According to the article, the over-35s group is a .... Facebook market.

    a) growing   **b)** steady   **c)** shrinking

64 MBA students at Haas first meet one another ....

    a) when they arrive   **b)** using the Haas intranet   **c)** on Facebook

65 Most Haas students and alumni use .... networking site.

    a) only their favourite   **b)** more than one   **c)** the BusinessBecause

WRITING

You work for a group of marketing consultants. Last week you gave a
presentation at a conference in Paris about marketing on the web. After
your talk, a man named Arno Dubrovsky came to talk to you and mentioned
that his company might be interested in hiring your services. Unfortunately,
you didn't have time to discuss his requirements in detail but he gave you
his business card.

**Write a letter of 100–150 words to Mr Dubrovsky, including the following
points:**

- Remind him about when and where you met.

- Apologise for not having more time to talk with him at the conference.

- Refer to his interest in your consultancy services.

- Refer to a brochure you are enclosing and your company's website: www.OnWeb.co.uk

- Point out that your company has a lot of experience in web marketing.

- Offer to phone or visit his company to discuss his company's needs.

Progress test 2 (Units 4–6)

A 🔊 4 **Listen to an employee appraisal interview. Match the sentence halves (1–5) to (a–e).**

1 When he took the job, Ahmed liked	a) a hard-working boss.
2 When Ahmed started work, he didn't have	b) the financial incentive.
3 Ahmed says he has	c) the world economy.
4 Ahmed's main motivation now is	d) the important job title.
5 Ahmed's only worry is	e) enough time off.

B 🔊 5 **Listen to another employee appraisal interview. Match the sentence halves (6–10) to (f–j).**

6 Howard feels that the company is	f) Howard's job satisfaction.
7 Howard likes	g) contact with people.
8 Howard says no one notices	h) working from home.
9 Sara wants to increase	i) a big machine.
10 Howard suggests that he might try	j) his contribution.

READING **A** **Read the article and decide if the statements are true (t) or false (f).**

Ask the experts: Be clear what you stand for

Rita Clifton, UK chairman of Interbrand, the branding consultancy:

"If you are to have a sustainable business, you need to think brand first and product second. If you don't have your unique angle indelibly attached to your products, your growth is going to be capped and you will eventually hit a product brick wall.

"The first and most important thing is that you have got to be clear about what you stand for and what makes you different. It is not just about defining yourself against the competition you might have today. You have to look forward.

"Kodak, for example, got obsessed with all its traditional competition. The business didn't think fast enough about what was coming down the line. That is a very big ask for small businesses but you have to have absolute clarity. So the second important element is clarity. If you have a brand that is all about reliability, it is no good at all if you fail to return calls or send scruffy people to clients.

"Thirdly, you cannot stand still. Innocent, another good example, was originally about smoothies but they are very restless. They are always looking further out to how they can bring healthy unadulterated food to people."

David Molian, director of the Business Growth and Development Programme at Cranfield School of Management:

"There is certainly something about understanding what it is you are fundamentally good at and therefore are able to replicate. That is not to say that a great business will only be good at one thing. Entrepreneurs can expand their capabilities, but there is something in this core area of competence that they stick to, which provides them with that winning formula.

"Sir Richard Branson, for instance, started off by being hugely successful in the music industry, then being successful in the airline business. The expansion of the Virgin brand into other areas, however, has been because of his ability to act as a mini-venture capitalist, picking the right sectors and the right people to back, where there is an opportunity to leverage the Virgin brand."

B **Now decide if the statements about the article on page 12 are true (t) or false (f).**

11 According to Rita Clifton, the product is more important than the brand.

12 Clifton says a product won't have long-term success if it isn't unique.

13 Kodak was successful because it looked to the future.

14 Innocent has succeeded because it hasn't stood still.

15 David Molian says that successful businesses must understand what they are good at.

16 Molian believes that great businesses are good at only one thing.

17 Most entrepreneurs succeed when they go beyond their core competence.

18 Richard Branson succeeded because he managed his brand well.

C **Read the article below. Choose the words and phrases (a–g) to complete the text.**

a) a problem

b) a risk-averse market

c) solutions to their problems

d) the answers

e) the competition

f) the emotional reason

g) the value

Ask the experts:
Ask questions and listen to answers

Mark Savinson, founder and managing director of Accredit, which helps companies measure and evaluate the effectiveness of their sales teams:

"Selling is a process of identifying someone with ....[19], confirming that they will spend money to address the problem, convincing them you can address the problem better than ....[20], and asking for the order.

"This is no different in ....[21] or in a boom market. What is different is whether you have to sell (the reality of a risk-averse market) or if you only had to have a product in the market and the buyer does the rest themselves.

"Remember, people like to buy, they do not like being sold to. Successful sales people and organisations recognise this and focus on getting the customer to realise they have an issue that can be addressed and ....[22] of addressing this issue is X. They then work with the customer to translate the identified value into reasons to buy.

"Finally, never forget that our customers are emotional human beings. Getting underneath ....[23] for wanting to solve a problem is key to winning business.

In difficult times, people do not necessarily want to buy a product – they want to buy ....[24], to put their mind at rest and to reduce dissatisfaction.

"We need to focus on the problems that keep our customers awake at night. We have to ask questions (and listen to ....[25]) to uncover the core issues. Finding these hot buttons will make us successful."

FINANCIAL TIMES

LANGUAGE **A** Complete the text with the correct verb tense (26–30).

Mobiles ring the changes in stores

JC Penney, the mid-price US department store chain, ...²⁶ (is cutting / cut) back somewhat on expenses last year, as its core middle-class shoppers were hit by the recession. But it did not stop spending on everything.

"We invested heavily in our digital initiatives," Mike Ullman, chief executive, ...²⁷ (told / had told) investors recently. "During the downturn, under the covers, there was a lot of heavy investment in building muscle to make sure we got a headstart in this."

JC Penney, with more than 1,000 stores, is at the leading edge of digital retailing. In February, for example, it held its monthly board meeting at Facebook's headquarters in California, where its board members were given a crash course in the potential of social networking.

The competition is only slightly behind JC Penny. Target, the US discount retailer, ...²⁸ (prepares / is preparing) to launch an entirely independent digital platform, ending its dependence on Amazon, the online marketplace which currently ....²⁹ (runs / ran) its website. Work on a new global e-commerce platform has been accelerated by Walmart, the world's largest retailer. Gap, the clothing retailer, is preparing to launch e-commerce businesses in western Europe, Canada and China.

"....................³⁰ (I've never seen / I never saw) a time like this in retail," says Andy Murray, head of Saatchi & Saatchi X, the in-store marketing agency that works with customers including Walmart and Procter & Gamble. "I think mobile is changing everything in retail."

Much of the initial attention has been focused on retailers embracing new digital marketing techniques aimed at mobile users, such as sending text messages, and using digital money-off coupons, and on steps to make their existing websites function on mobile browsers. But retailers are also facing a world that has been changed by the fact that shoppers will now increasingly be online, via their phones, even as they visit a physical store. They will expect a unified shopping experience.

FINANCIAL TIMES

B Find five examples of passive verbs in the text.

31 ....

32 ....

33 ....

34 ....

35 ....

C Find adverbs in the text with the following meanings.

36 more than a little ....

37 a lot ....

38 a small amount ....

39 completely ....

40 more and more ....

SKILLS   **A**   Complete the conversation with the appropriate phrase (a–j).

a) I don't want to repeat myself but   f) So what you're saying is

b) Hold on now   g) Are you saying

c) I want to ask a question.   h) I'd like to make a suggestion.

d) if you give us $2,500 next week   i) I'm sorry to say

e) providing you can   j) how do you feel

Dean: We agreed a budget of $15,000.

Alan: Right. But we've had some unexpected costs.

Dean: ....[41] that you need more than that.

Alan: Yes, ...[42] I've been saying for the last six months that we simply don't have any more money for this.

Alan: ....[43] that you don't have the money, or that you don't want to spend it?

Dean: ....[44] I think we should leave this point and come back to it later.

Alan: ....[45], don't you think we need to sort this out before we talk about anything else?

Dean: Bianca, ...[46] about this?

Bianca: Well, ...,[47] I agree with Alan on this one. We need to talk through it.

Alan: Thanks, Bianca. Dean, ...[48] we can deliver the machines, and we'll give your employees training on them. That wasn't part of the original agreement, but we can do that.

Dean: ....[49] What date are you offering to do the installation?

Alan: We can agree to installation on 12 August, ...[50] give us the extra money.

B   Match Beatrice's sentences (a–e) to Carlos's sentences to complete the conversation.

a) I was wondering if you'd be interested in talking with us about a job.

b) I wonder if we could talk about it? ADG are offering a top salary with very good benefits, and they give staff a substantial bonus – well above the industry average. Could we get together?

c) Hello Mr Ortega. My name's Beatrice Lumb. I work for R&S, the executive recruitment agency. I was given your name by Kim Mason.

d) OK, I quite understand.

e) Kim thought you might consider looking at a position that's become vacant at ADG Logistics.

Carlos: Carlos Ortega speaking.

Beatrice: ....[51]

Carlos: Oh, hello. What can I do for you?

Beatrice: ....[52]

Carlos: Oh, yes?

Beatrice: ....[53]

Carlos: I'm flattered that you've called, but I'm very happy in my job.

Beatrice: ....[54]

Carlos: I'm afraid there's no point in us meeting. I'm completely happy where I am now.

Beatrice: ....[55]

VOCABULARY

A Match the prefixes (56–60) to the words (a–e).

56 em   a) perform

57 under   b) regulate

58 dis   c) lateral

59 de   d) loyal

60 bi   e) power

B Choose the correct word from Exercise A to complete the sentences.

61 It was .... of John to tell our competitors about the new product launch.

62 The government is going to .... the sector in the near future.

63 We don't need someone who's going to .... the way Leon did. We need someone who can sell!

64 The two countries agreed to work hard to improve .... relations.

65 If you .... employees – give them real control over their work – that increases productivity.

WRITING

You represent a firm of venture capitalists. You have investigated three new businesses that are all seeking venture capital funding. You should recommend the one that is the least risky and offers the best prospects for a good return on your investment.

Using the notes below, write a memo of 200–250 words to the new business funding committee. Give a brief assessment of each business and end with your recommendation.

404G4

A group of young computer professionals have devised a new computer game and want to market it.

Game is fun and creative. The group has lots of other ideas.

Will be difficult to enter this market – highly competitive.

PoshRide

An existing company – offers luxury chauffeur-driven car hire to companies.

Two partners – committed and ambitious. Strong customer base established.

They want to expand – open regional offices. Expansion often difficult but prospects good if managed well.

Partners have demonstrated good business skills.

I-rec

Electronics engineer invented a security device based on eye recognition – seeks funding to manufacture and market it.

Invention is effective – should have a good market.

Not yet patented.

Inventor has no business experience.

Progress test 3 (Units 7–9)

A 🔊 **6 Listen to a presentation by Lydia Jones, a cabin crew trainer at A–Z Airlines. Choose the best answer, a, b or c, for each question.**

1   What is the topic of Lydia's presentation?
    a)   the company's benefits package
    b)   on-the-job teamwork
    c)   the basic training offered by the airline

2   Who is she speaking to?
    a)   a group of new employees
    b)   the team responsible for training new employees
    c)   a group of experienced managers

3   How many key elements are there to teamwork?
    a)   three
    b)   four
    c)   five

4   What does Lydia say every team needs?
    a)   clear rules
    b)   well-defined roles for team members
    c)   a leader

5   Which skill does she say is important for a team leader?
    a)   to be authoritarian
    b)   to be ruthless when it's necessary
    c)   to be decisive

6   What does she say about knowledge and skills?
    a)   That the new employees already have some knowledge and skills.
    b)   That knowledge and skill can only be developed on the job.
    c)   That employees become fully trained in the first year of work.

7   What does she say about rules?
    a)   The airline's rules are designed to stop bad or dangerous behaviour.
    b)   Everyone must follow the rules or they risk being sacked.
    c)   Rules create an efficient working environment.

8   Which of these benefits of having clear rules does she mention?
    a)   Rules help reinforce the role of the team leader.
    b)   Following rules contributes to safety.
    c)   Rules help reduce serious communication problems.

9   What does she say about mistakes?
    a)   The job of the team is to reduce mistakes.
    b)   Mistakes happen.
    c)   It's important for people to take responsibility for their mistakes.

10 What does Lydia say is important about relationships among team members?
    a)   Open communication is essential.
    b)   A little friendly competition can be helpful.
    c)   The only practical way to do the job is to concentrate on your own work.

READING **A** **Read the article and identify the paragraph (i–vii) in which you can find information about the following:**

11 What Mike Lynch said about the state of the UK economy.

12 What business and enterprise minister Mark Prisk says about the economy.

13 A comparison of venture capital funds in 2008 and 2009.

14 How politicians will react to the Nesta report.

15 What venture capitalists did in 2009.

16 What Nesta believes about the future and what investors should do now.

17 What the National Endowment for Science, Technology and the Arts has recently said about the venture capital industry.

Venture capital hit by 'slump' in funding

i) The venture capital industry has 'slumped' after the credit crunch, according to the National Endowment for Science, Technology and the Arts. Investment in start-ups specialising in new technology has fallen 40 per cent in value over two years. Fundraising by venture capital companies has dropped 50 per cent to levels below those following the 2000 dotcom crash.

ii) The report from Nesta, an independent body funded by a Lottery endowment, will make discouraging reading for politicians hoping that innovation will help stimulate economic recovery. The reduction in access to funding means that fewer technology companies are likely to bring lucrative new products to market. The UK fell behind France in venture capital investment last year, reflecting weaker tax incentives.

iii) Mike Lynch, chairman of Nesta's investment committee and founder of Autonomy, a quoted software business valued at £4.4bn, said the debilitated state of UK venture capital was partly cyclical but added: 'There is a structural change that is more worrying. Venture capital firms that would have been happy investing £1m-£2m in a start-up have shifted to backing £100m private equity deals.' Mr Lynch said Apax, an early backer of Autonomy, "doesn't do that sort of deal any more". The Nesta chairman said venture-backed businesses were the feedstock from which big, successful technology companies grew. "It is hard to know how the economy will do well without a significant number of know-how-based companies in the FTSE 100." He added that only two FTSE 100 companies – Autonomy and chip designer Arm – currently met those criteria and "we need another five or six".

iv) During 2009, venture capitalists invested just £677m in UK start-ups, a 27 per cent decline and the smallest amount for a decade. The number of investments fell 17 per cent to 266. New companies had the worst difficulties finding capital. 'Early-stage funding', as investment for these fragile fledglings is called, dropped 53 per cent by value.

v) Mark Prisk, business and enterprise minister, said on Wednesday: "The government recognises the importance of high-growth, innovative companies to the UK economy and the problems they can encounter accessing venture capital. That's why in last month's Budget we announced a new Enterprise Capital Fund to target innovative start-ups and a Growth Capital Fund to invest in small businesses needing venture finance to grow."

vi) Only 11 venture capital funds were able to raise capital in 2009 compared with 22 in 2008. Investors provided £574m, 64 per cent less than the year before. Institutions have been discouraged from investing in venture capital by its high risks and low returns. The collapse of dotcom investments earlier in the decade triggered heavy losses. Returns have been better over a 10-year period, with 54 per cent of UK exits recovering one to five times investors' outlays, compared with 27 per cent that failed to break even.

vii) Nesta, which is a significant venture investor, is optimistic about the future. The company believes we have reached the low point in venture capital's fortunes and that growth will soon return. As the economy recovers, exits through flotations and trade sales should increase, allowing companies to recycle profits into new investments and attract new institutional backers. Mr Lynch said: "This is the best time to invest because you can get in at a good price. In contrast, at the top of the cycle the number of good companies is the same but a lot more money is chasing them."

FINANCIAL TIMES

B **Now decide if these statements are true (t) or false (f).**

18 Venture capital companies are raising more money now than they were after the 2000 dotcom crash.

19 Technology companies will find it more difficult to raise finance.

20 Mike Lynch started the company called Autonomy.

21 Lynch says that venture capital firms now avoid £100m deals and prefer much smaller ones.

22 In 2009, there were only 17 investments in UK start-ups.

23 The government doesn't think start-ups are very important to the UK economy.

24 In 2008, investors put up more than £1bn in capital.

25 Mike Lynch thinks investors should wait until the economy improves before investing.

LANGUAGE **A** **Read the text below. Say what the numbered words (26–30) refer to.**

26 ....

27 ....

28 ....

29 ....

30 ....

Ralph Schlosstein

Ralph Schlosstein, chief executive of Evercore, the independent advisory firm, is not a man who has spent much time talking about himself. He's more
5 accustomed to being a supporting player than taking the leading role. As a co-founder of BlackRock, now the world's largest money manager, he[26] played president to Larry Fink's chief
10 executive for two decades until his departure in 2008. It[27] was clearly a role

he enjoyed. "As I[28] actually said at my goodbye dinner, there was not a single day where I sat there and thought, 'I
15 wish you[29] weren't here and I wish I had the job'" he says. "First, we[30] had a great partnership and second, [Larry] does a phenomenal job as the chief executive of BlackRock."

FT FINANCIAL TIMES

B **Write the most appropriate modal verb (positive or negative) in each gap. The meaning is given in brackets.**

31 I .... have taken the train but the last one had left, so I got a taxi. (If there had been a train ...)

32 You .... have ordered more paper for the copier. I'd already ordered it. (It wasn't necessary.)

33 They .... have left the office already. It's only 3 p.m. (It's impossible.)

34 There were only two people who could have written this note. It wasn't Axel, so it .... have been Victoria. (It could only have been.)

35 You .... have gone to the presentation on database management. It was great! (It was recommended.)

C **Complete the text with the prepositions in the box.**

about in of to to

Kristjan Hiiemaa is co-founder ....[36] Erply, a software company in Estonia. Like a lot of entrepreneurs, he has great ideas but
5 lacks access ....[37] the money he needs to turn his dreams into reality. Hiiemaa has pitched his ideas ....[38] Saul Klein of Index Ventures, one of Europe's technology

10 venture capital firms. Klein is optimistic ....[39] Erply's future and plans to invest ....[40] the new business, in the hope of getting a big return in the future.

VOCABULARY

A **Match four of the five managers below with the team where they will be best suited.**

Susan: creative, inspiring, diplomatic

Matt: decisive, competent, responsible

Benny: sociable, loyal, considerate, logical

Stella: supportive, sociable, flexible

Ian: organised, efficient, logical

41 We have some brilliant and creative people in our team but we're not always good at handling everyday routines. We need someone to remind us about what to do and when – someone who knows where everything is kept, and can suggest the best way to do things.

Person: ....

42 Ideally, our new team member should enjoy working with people and should get on well with others. He or she should be able to explain things clearly to customers. And – as our work is never routine – it is important to be able to adapt quickly to changing situations.

Person: ....

43 The ideal candidate must be able to deal with all kinds of difficult situations, and take control when something goes wrong. He or she must be able to keep a clear head and not get distracted when things happen fast. Because this person will manage a large team and a large budget, he or she must be sensible and able to make good judgements.

Person: ....

44 We need someone who can produce new and effective ideas and can give other people a feeling of excitement and a desire to do something great. This person also needs to deal politely and skilfully with our team of artists and designers without upsetting them.

Person: ....

B **Choose the correct word, a, b or c, to complete each sentence.**

45 The seminar starts at 10:00 but we're having a .... breakfast at 8:30.

    a) pre-seminar   **b)** post-seminar   **c)** pro-seminar

46 We need to improve our training to .... staff turnover.

    a) build   **b)** inspire   **c)** reduce

47 Everyone worked hard last year, but then in January everyone lost motivation. Let's think of a way to .... everyone and increase sales again.

    a) demotivate   **b)** remotivate   **c)** hypermotivate

48 We'll finally be in the black next year, after we're repaid our ....

    a) grant   **b)** dividend   **c)** loan

49 When we began, we got our .... capital from friends and family.

    a) credit   **b)** start-up   **c)** asset

50 We .... on the loan when we missed our January payment.

    a) overpaid   **b)** defaulted   **c)** ripped off

Answer key

Entry test

Listening (10 marks)

1 Japan (accept Tokyo)
2 Thursday, Friday
3 Wednesday afternoon at two o'clock
4 That it's OK with everyone
5 lunchtime on Wednesday
6 9:30 on Wednesday morning
7 the briefing meeting
8 as soon as possible
9 rescheduled for next week
10 after lunch/later

Language (15 marks)

11 opened
12 exchanged
13 has taken
14 offers
15 place
16 is
17 has
18 have
19 have developed
20 being
21 e   22 a   23 d   24 b   25 c

Vocabulary (15 marks)

26 grow
27 resign
28 decline
29 boost
30 remain
31 journey
32 company
33 distribution
34 products
35 effect
36 details
37 document
38 copy
39 region
40 yourselves

Reading (10 marks)

41 F   42 T   43 T   44 F   45 F
46 b   47 c   48 a   49 e   50 d

Writing (15 marks)

See page 43 for examiner's guidelines.

Speaking (15 marks)

See page 42 for examiner's guidelines.

Model answer to writing task

Dear Mr James,

Many thanks for sending details of your travel arrangements. Our driver will come to the airport to meet you. He will be carrying a sign with your name on it.

I have now booked a room for you at the Metro Hotel. Our company normally uses this hotel and I think you will find it very comfortable and quiet. It is just 10 minutes' walk from our offices. I have informed the hotel you will be arriving late.

I will come to your hotel on Tuesday morning to meet you and walk with you to our offices. I hope 8:45 won't be too early for you.

I wish you a pleasant trip and look forward to meeting you next Tuesday.

Yours sincerely,

Progress test 1

Listening (10 marks)

1 a   2 b   3 b   4 a   5 c
6 Darren (Sorry, I didn't quite catch that.)
7 Liz (What do you mean by really bad?)
8 Liz (Sorry, I'm not sure I know what you mean.)
9 Liz (Could you explain that in more detail?)
10 Darren (Sorry, it's a terrible connection. Can I call you back?)

Language (15 marks)

11 grapevine
12 bush
13 nutshell
14 stick
15 wall
16 off
17 up
18 off
19 up
20 on
21 marketing
22 sales
23 product
24 campaign
25 loyalty

Vocabulary (10 marks)

26 marketing
27 product
28 market
29 identity
30 underperformed
31 misjudged
32 customer
33 focus
34 sensitive
35 articulate

Skills (15 marks)

36 c   37 h   38 a   39 g
40 b   41 f   42 e   43 d

44 The purpose of the/our meeting this morning is to discuss our/the marketing strategy.
45 That's the best idea I've heard for a long time.
46 We want all your ideas, however crazy you think they are.
47 Any other ideas about what we can do about this?
48 I was thinking maybe we should go to New York City.
49 We could just go for a four-star hotel in Manhattan.
50 Yes, that's a good idea, because it will save money.

Reading (15 marks)

51 F   52 T   53 F   54 F   55 T   56 T
57 F   58 T   59 b   60 a   61 c   62 a
63 a   64 c   65 b

Writing (15 marks)

See page 43 for examiner's guidelines.

Model answer to writing task

Dear Mr Dubrovsky,

It was good to meet you at the conference in Paris last week. I am very sorry that I had to leave early and did not have more time to talk to you at the conference.

You mentioned that your company might be interested in hiring our consulting services. I am enclosing our most recent brochure so that you can learn more about us and what we can offer. You may also like to visit our website at www.OnWeb.co.uk. As you can see, we have a lot of experience in marketing on the Web and have helped many businesses to launch successful campaigns.

If you would like to discuss your company's needs in more detail, I would be pleased to call you at any time, or to visit you at your office.

Yours sincerely,

Progress test 2

Listening (10 marks)

1 d   2 e   3 a   4 b   5 c
6 i   7 g   8 j   9 f   10 h

Reading (15 marks)

11 F   12 F   13 F   14 T   15 T
16 F   17 F   18 T   19 a   20 e
21 b   22 g   23 f   24 c   25 d

Language (15 marks)

26 cut
27 told
28 is preparing
29 runs
30 I've never seen
31 were hit by
32 were given
33 has been accelerated
34 has been focused on
35 has been changed
36 somewhat
37 heavily
38 slightly
39 entirely
40 increasingly

Skills (15 marks)

41 f   42 a   43 g   44 h   45 b
46 j   47 i   48 d   49 c   50 e
51 c   52 a   53 e   54 b   55 d

Vocabulary (10 marks)

56 e   57 a   58 d   59 b   60 c
61 disloyal
62 deregulate
63 underperform
64 bilateral
65 empower

Writing (15 marks)

See page 43 for examiner's guidelines.

Model answer to writing task

Memo

To: New business funding committee

From : (name)

I have investigated three new businesses that are seeking venture capital funding and this is my assessment of each business.

404G4 is a computer game developed by a group of young computer professionals. The game is creative and fun and the group seem to have a lot of other ideas. However, this is a highly competitive market and it will be difficult for them to enter. This would also be a high risk investment for us.

PoshRide is an existing company that offers chauffeur-driven luxury car hire to companies. The two partners are very committed and ambitious and have already established a strong customer base. They now want to expand by opening regional offices. Expansion can be difficult but prospects for growth are good if they manage it well. Their success so far demonstrates good business skills.

I-rec us a security device based on eye recognition. It is the invention of an electronics engineer who wants to manufacture and market it to companies. It should have a good market if developed in the right way. However, the inventor has not yet patented the device, and also lacks business experience. For these reasons, I feel that this venture would be too risky for us at this time.

Conclusion

My conclusion is that the venture which offers us the least risk and the best prospects of a good return is PoshRide. I therefore recommend that we invest funds in this business.

Progress test 3

Listening *(10 marks)*

1 b   2 a   3 b   4 c   5 c
6 a   7 c   8 b   9 b   10 a

Reading *(15 marks)*

11 iii   12 v   13 vi   14 ii   15 iv
16 vii   17 i   18 F   19 T   20 T
21 F   22 F   23 F   24 T   25 F

Language *(15 marks)*

26 Ralph Schlosstein
27 president (of BlackRock)
28 Ralph Schlosstein
29 Larry Fink
30 Ralph Schlosstein and Larry Fink
31 would
32 needn't
33 can't
34 must
35 should
36 of
37 to
38 to
39 about
40 in

Vocabulary *(10 marks)*

41 Ian
42 Stella
43 Matt
44 Susan
45 a   46 c   47 b   48 c   49 b   50 b

Skills *(15 marks)*

51 d   52 a   53 e   54 b   55 c
56 My main concern
57 I know
58 I don't think
59 How do you think
60 One thing you could do
61 Why do you
62 Do you have
63 Let's look at
64 I'm sorry
65 Let's see

Writing *(15 marks)*

See page 43 for Examiner's guidelines.

Model answer to writing task

A comparative study of teamwork in Poland and Sweden

Background

(As given)

Purpose

The purpose of the study was to identify areas of difference which could lead to friction, and to make recommendations for facilitating better cooperation between the teams.

Method

The study was conducted over a period of two weeks, during which time our consultants closely followed each team and made observations on patterns of communication and decision-making.

Findings

It was observed that the Polish team work as individuals and each engineer is highly specialised. They rarely hold meetings but communicate mainly through the team leader, who coordinates and directs the work. Much of the communication is by e-mail.

The Swedish team, on the other hand, work as a group, hold frequent meetings and communicate face-to-face. Engineers are more generalised and ideas are created through brainstorming and cooperation. Decisions are reached by consensus within the team.

Conclusions

It is clear that the two teams have very different working patterns. This could lead to serious problems and the success of the joint venture could be at risk as a result. It will be important, therefore, to establish a common approach. We strongly recommend that, before the project starts up, the teams are brought together to discuss their differences and to agree on the ground rules for future cooperation. In addition, a programme of team-building activities could be set up to facilitate better cooperation between the teams.

Progress test 4

Listening *(10 marks)*

1 home
2 new
3 caused
4 happened
5 doesn't work
6 clarify
7 schedule another visit
8 shows
9 understands
10 will

Vocabulary *(10 marks)*

11 buck
12 straw
13 mile
14 bottom
15 press
16 damage
17 action
18 bid
19 venture
20 stake

Reading *(15 marks)*

21 a   22 c   23 b   24 a   25 c
26 b   27 b   28 c   29 a   30 b
31 b   32 a   33 a   34 c   35 c

Skills *(15 marks)*

36 c   37 h   38 i   39 g   40 b
41 f   42 a   43 e   44 d   45 b
46 e   47 a   48 d   49 f   50 c

Language *(15 marks)*

51 producing
52 to speak
53 telling
54 watching
55 to switch off
56 have
57 they'll
58 gave
59 wouldn't have gone
60 were
61 may work
62 be working
63 going to work
64 will work
65 the work

Writing *(15 marks)*

See page 43 for examiner's guidelines.

Model answer to writing task

At about four o'clock on Tuesday 5 July, there was an explosion and fire at Acomb Chemicals, Hawley factory. The factory produces paint. Workers at the plant activated the fire alarm, and the fire brigade arrived within ten minutes. The firemen put the fire out by five o'clock. Two workers from the factory were taken to hospital with difficulty breathing. There were no other injuries.

There are no houses near the fire but roads in the area have been closed while the company tests the air quality in the area. All of the workers who were in the factory at the time have been checked by doctors and sent home. No problems have been found among the workers. Employees who would have started their shift at nine o'clock this morning have been told to stay home today while the factory is made safe.

The cause of the fire is being investigated, but at this point it is not considered suspicious. Further, it does not appear as though any dangerous chemicals were involved in the accident.

When the fire broke out, the workers followed the correct procedures to the letter. The fire brigade confirmed that the workers' quick response stopped the fire from spreading, avoiding a much bigger problem.

For additional information on the company, visit our website: acombchem.com

or contact Rita Mercer on +44 (0)190-788-322.

Date: 5 July

Title: Explosion and fire at paint factory under control

Addressed to: the press

Author: (Student's name)

Exit test

Listening *(10 marks)*

1 b	2 c	3 a	4 b	5 c
6 b	7 a	8 b	9 c	10 a

Skills *(10 marks)*

11 g	12 c	13 h	14 a	15 i
16 b	17 j	18 e	19 f	20 d

Vocabulary *(10 marks)*

21 persuasive
22 customer
23 disrupted
24 brand
25 severance payment
26 significantly
27 considerate
28 debtors
29 refunds
30 joint venture

Reading *(10 marks)*

31 c	32 e	33 j	34 d	35 h
36 i	37 g	38 f	39 a	40 b

Language *(10 marks)*

41 surprised
42 exceptionally
43 gone up
44 caused
45 than
46 were
47 goes
48 about
49 sales
50 to rise

Writing *(15 marks)*

See page 43 for examiner's guidelines.

Speaking *(15 marks)*

See page 42 for examiner's guidelines.

Model answer to writing task

Subject: New heating and cooling system for warehouse

We need to purchase a new heating and cooling system for the warehouse and I have investigated three systems, all of which would suit our purposes from a technical point of view.

As can be seen in the attached table, **System A** has the lowest purchase cost. However, the running costs for this system are high at €4,100 a year. In addition, the guarantee for this system is only one year, which means we would have to pay a further €850 per year for a service contract after this guarantee has expired.

System B has a higher purchase cost than System A and also a higher running cost. This would be the most expensive option for us.

System C has the highest purchase cost. However, it is a new system which offers a high level of energy efficiency. The running cost for a year is only €2,900, which would compensate for the higher purchase cost after four years. Moreover, this system has a five-year guarantee, which means we would not have to pay for a service contract during the first five years after purchase. The overall cost over five years is €6,000 cheaper for this system than for System A.

Conclusion and recommendation

My conclusion is the System C offer the best value and efficiency and I recommend that we buy this system.

SKILLS **A** **Match the halves of the sentences (51–55) to (a–e) from a presentation.**

51 The purpose of my talk today is to

52 As I'm sure you're all

53 However, the new offices

54 Please

55 The town centre location will

a) aware, the move will mean we all have slightly less space.

b) look at the slide, which shows a map of the area.

c) give us easy access to some of our most important clients.

d) explain our plans for moving to our new offices next month.

e) have many outstanding features, including big windows with lots of natural light.

B **Complete these conversations with the phrases in the box.**

| Do you have   How do you think   I don't think   I know   I'm sorry |
| Let's look at   Let's see   My main concern   One thing you could do   Why do you |

Conversation 1

Max: ....[56] is the working schedule. Why am I always working on Friday nights?

Ann: ....[57] how you feel. It's not a very good time to work. It might be worth asking some of the other guys if they want to switch nights with you.

Max: ....[58] that's the answer. No one wants to work on a Friday night!

Ann: ....[59] we should deal with this, then?

Max: ....[60] is put someone else on Friday nights!

Conversation 2

Abdullah: ....[61] need a loan?

Heinz: We need to hire two new software technicians so we can launch the product quickly.

Abdullah: ....[62] any other backers?

Heinz: Right now, no.

Abdullah: ....[63] this another way. What if we made it a share purchase instead of a loan?

Heinz: I don't know. We'd sell you 50,000 shares at $2.00 a share. I know that's high, but ...

Abdullah: ....[64], we can't go that high.

Heinz: OK, fine. But I still think we can work something out. ....[65] what we've got so far.

Read the first paragraph of a summary of a consultant's report below, and the notes underneath it. Then write the rest of the summary using the sub-headings and information given. You should write about 200–250 words.

A comparative study of team work in Poland and Sweden

Background

Company X (Swedish) and Company Y (Polish) are to set up a joint venture in which a team of software engineers from each company will work together to build a state-of-the-art heating system control unit. I've been asked to carry out a study into the working patterns of teams in each company.

Purpose
Identify areas of difference > possible friction
Make recommendation (how to improve cooperation between teams?)

Method
Two week study period: consultants followed teams, observed patterns of communication and decision-making

Findings
Polish team:
· work as individuals
· engineers specialised
· meetings rare
· communication via e-mail or through team leader
· leader coordinates and directs

Swedish team:
· work as a group
· engineers more generalised
· meetings frequent
· brainstorm ideas together
· communication face-to-face
· decisions by consensus

Conclusion
Very different! > serious problems possible > joint venture at risk
Important to establish common approach

Progress test 4 (Units 10–12)

A 🔊 7 **Listen to a phone conversation between Susan, a customer, and Martin, a customer service representative. Choose the correct word(s) to complete each sentence.**

1 Susan has a problem with her (home / mobile) telephone.

2 Susan is a (long-time / new) customer of Martin's company.

3 Susan says the engineer (repaired / caused) the problem.

4 Martin asks Susan to explain what (happened / made her angry).

5 The problem is that one of her telephones (is missing / doesn't work).

6 Martin wants to (clarify / summarise) that the engineer left without repairing the phone.

7 The engineer told Susan she needed (to schedule another visit / write a letter of complaint).

8 Martin (shows / doesn't show) empathy.

9 Martin (doesn't understand / understands) the problem very well.

10 Martin (will / won't) try to solve the problem today.

VOCABULARY **A** **Complete the sentences with the words in the box.**

action   bid   bottom   buck   damage   mile   press   stake   straw   venture

11 I'm not going to pass the .... I intend to take responsibility for my actions.

12 His rude remarks are the last .... I simply can't work with him any more.

13 Not only did he get the work in on time, he went the extra .... and delivered it by hand.

14 We need to get to the .... of why the G-225 keeps breaking down.

15 We have to hold a .... conference and explain what's going on.

16 At this point, we just need to do .... limitation and not let the situation get any worse!

17 If they decide to take legal ...., we're going to have a big problem.

18 MPPC has launched a takeover .... for Pierpont Ripley and Company.

19 The two French companies have set up a joint .... in Vietnam.

20 We've just bought a 50% .... is Laovitech Group.

A **Read the article.**

Learning from crime

In a non-descript room in the Ecole Militaire, a military training centre in Paris, a team of six men and a woman sit in intense discussion. As their company's crisis management team, they have been informed that 10 colleagues, including their chief executive, have been kidnapped at the opening ceremony of a production plant in Colombia. Within seconds, the company's security chief in Bogota is on the phone; "It looks like it could be the Farc [the Marxist Colombian rebel group]. It's a hell of a mess here." For the next half hour the seven discuss options and make plans, while answering calls from within the company as well as from the French authorities, the media and anxious customers. Then Bogota calls again with the news they feared. "We had a call from a guy calling himself José. He says the Farc are detaining the hostages and they want $6m ransom."

Fortunately, the kidnapping is an exercise and the seven are all students – although they have considerable management experience – in the first intake of a one-year criminal risk management programme designed by Edhec, the French business school with campuses in Nice, Paris and Lille. "They are all so into it. And some of these people have already worked in crisis situations. I'm amazed myself [at the involvement]," says Bertrand Monnet, head of Edhec's research centre into criminal risk management and the professor behind the programme.

Nicolas Krmic, a security manager with Acergy, an equipment supplier to the oil and gas industry, faces threats including kidnapping, data theft and armed robbery on a daily basis in his work in Nigeria and other African states. "Security did not use to be a [core] business topic for most companies. But we have to understand that to win business you must deal with it. And if you prove reliable, clients will want to deal with you again." This dovetails with the thinking at Edhec. "This is not only about crisis management, but about risk management as a whole. It's not just another add-on, it's a whole philosophy which we apply from our financial research centre to the programmes in the teaching rooms. This is a strategic option for our school, for students at all levels," says Pierre-Guy Hourquet, dean of executive programmes.

Reactions from the pioneer students are very positive. Pierre-Yves Arnaud, a security consultant, has worked in the field with oil companies in Nigeria and Chad. In spite of such a wealth of practical experience, he says the programme has given him a better analytical understanding of risk and "a methodology to apply in any situation" for assessment. "I should have started [my career] with this," he says. He says he now better understands what he calls "the strategic importance of communications" in a crisis. "Whether you technically succeed or not, if you have a good communication with media, you will 'win' the case," he says.

The security services also value co-operation with the school. "When we mount an operation, for example, to release hostages, it is to our advantage that that top management in companies know us a little bit and understand what we do and how we work. This is why we work with Edhec," says Lieutenant-Colonel Franck Chaix, commander of the Intervention Force of the GIGN, the French anti-terrorist unit.

FINANCIAL TIMES

B **Choose the best word or phrase, a, b or c, to complete the sentences.**

21 In the first paragraph, the seven people are .... a crisis situation.
a) analysing
b) writing a press release about
c) inventing

22 The crisis is ....
a) an explosion at a plant
b) a terrorist attack
c) a kidnapping

23 The seven people are .... taking a course.
a) college students
b) experienced managers
c) security guards

24 The people discussing the crisis ....
a) are very serious about it
b) are not interested in it
c) don't know it's practice

25 The Edhec criminal risk management course lasts ....
  a) one week
  b) one month
  c) one year

26 Bertrand Monnet is ....
  a) a security manager
  b) a professor
  c) a student at Edhec

27 Acergy is .... company.
  a) a security
  b) an equipment supply
  c) a consulting

28 Nicolas Krmic ....
  a) used to be a business student
  b) teaches at Edhec
  c) manages crises every day

29 Krmic says that security .... a core business topic.
  a) has become
  b) has always been
  c) may never be

30 Risk management involves .... crises.
  a) releasing information about
  b) predicting and preparing for
  c) always avoiding

31 Pierre-Guy Hourquet says that risk management and crisis management ....
  a) should be treated as separate, special fields
  b) should be included as part of business philosophy
  c) is very difficult to master

32 Pierre-Yves Arnaud .... the Edhec course.
  a) has taken
  b) may enrol in
  c) doesn't approve of

33 Arnaud .... practical experience in crisis management.
  a) has a lot of
  b) wants to get more
  c) has very little

34 Arnaud says that .... is one of the most important parts of crisis management.
  a) ability to work under stress
  b) contingency planning
  c) good media communications

35 The security services think the training at Edhec is .... for managers.
  a) dangerous
  b) confusing
  c) useful

SKILLS **A** **Tom Adams is a spokesperson for an oil company. He's giving a press conference. Complete the sentences with the words and phrases (a–i).**

a) you saying that

b) you be more specific

c) happened

d) answer it this way

e) an interesting question

f) not sure I know the answer

g) anyone like to ask

h) are we doing

i) can you expect

Tom: OK, welcome to the press conference. I'm here tonight to tell you about the accident we've had at South Beach, and to tell you what we're doing about it. I'll tell you what happened, what we're doing now and what you can expect to happen in the next week.

OK, what .... [36]? At two o'clock this morning, an oil tanker, the *Southern Sun*, hit rocks near South Beach in a storm. The tanker was damaged. There is some oil leaking into the sea.

Right, what .... [37] about it? We already have more than 100 people working in the area. We've used special equipment to stop the oil from coming on to the beach.

What .... [38] in the next week? We will take the boat off the rocks, probably as soon as tonight. We will skim most of the oil off the surface of the water. We will be prepared to clean up any oil that reaches the beach very, very quickly. Would .... [39] any questions?

Reporter 1: You said there's some oil leaking into the sea. Could .... [40]?

Tom: Sorry, I'm .... [41] to that one.

Reporter 2: Are .... [42] you don't know how much oil is in the water?

Tom: That's .... [43]. Let me .... [44]. We know how much oil was in the tanker yesterday. Tonight, we will know exactly how much has spilled.

B **Match the sentences (45–50) with a response (a–f).**

45 We're aiming for 100% reliability.

46 We've had a 100% increase in sales this quarter over last quarter.

47 It was kind of funny. We had food for 20 people but 100 came to the reception!

48 I think I have a good idea about things.

49 Ian is 20 minutes late! I feel really angry!

50 Excuse me, I have a question.

a) How did you deal with it?

b) 100%? Do you think you can do that?

c) How can I help?

d) Could you be more specific?

e) So you're saying that sales have doubled?

f) I'm not surprised you're upset.

LANGUAGE

A **Choose the correct form of the verb in brackets to complete the sentences.**

51 The company stopped .... (produce) cigarettes in 1995, but they still manufacture candy.

52 When my computer broke, I tried .... (speak) to someone in technical support, but I couldn't get through.

53 I regret .... (tell) Joe that I was unhappy at work. He told my boss what I'd said!

54 Mr Pile became a successful investor by carefully .... (watch) other traders and learning from their mistakes.

55 I didn't remember .... (switch off) my computer when I left the office, so it was on all weekend.

B **Choose the correct word(s) to complete each sentence.**

56 If you (will have / have) time, come and see me.

57 If they make their target, (they'll / they would) have a big party.

58 If we (will give / gave) them a 25% discount, they'd double their order.

59 If I'd understood how serious the problem was, I (wouldn't have gone / didn't go) on holiday.

60 If I (am / were) you, I'd tell Dirk that he should do his own research.

C **Complete the sentences with the words in the box.**

| be working   going to work   may work   the work   will work |

61 I .... for another three years before I'm promoted.

62 We'll .... in our new offices next January.

63 We're .... on improving our image next season.

64 It's highly likely that Bev .... from home as of next month.

65 There's no chance of .... finishing this week.

WRITING **A** **You work in the public relations office of a large chemical manufacturing firm. There has been an accident at one of your factories. Use the information below and write a press release of 200–250 words for the news media. Include the following points:**

- A header that makes clear who it comes from, what the subject is and which part of the press it is aimed at.

- A subject line.

- At the end: date, title, 'addressed to', and author.

Acomb Chemicals

Tuesday 5 July

- explosion and fire at Hawley Factory (paint factory) under control
- about 4:00 this morning: explosion and fire
- workers activated fire alarm
- fire brigade arrived w/in ten minutes
- firemen put the fire out by 5:00
- two workers - hospital (difficulty breathing) but no other injuries
- no houses near the fire
- roads in area closed while company tests the air quality
- workers in the factory at the time have been checked by doctors - home (no problems found)
- employees who would have started their shift at 9:00 told stay home today while the factory made safe
- cause being investigated
- not considered suspicious
- does not appear as though any dangerous chemicals involved
- workers followed the correct procedures to the letter
- fire brigade confirmed workers' quick response stopped fire spreading, avoiding much bigger problem
- More info – acombchem.com – contact Rita Mercer on +44 (0)190-788-322

Exit test (General review)

◄》 8 **Listen to an interview with Vic Wurzel, CEO of Chapman Laney, a financial services firm. Choose the best word(s), a, b or c, to complete these sentences.**

1 Vic Wurzel arrived at Chapman Laney .... a crisis.
   a) before   b) during   c) after

2 Chapman Laney was originally ....
   a) a management consultant   b) an investment bank   c) a corporate advisor

3 Chapman Laney had problems because it took too many ....
   a) risks   b) loans   c) losses

4 When he arrived, Wurzel .... 500 employees.
   a) fired   b) hired   c) transferred

5 Chapman Laney was founded in ....
   a) 19**35**   b) 19**45**   c) 1954

6 Wurzel wants to .... the risk his company takes.
   a) increase   b) decrease   c) maintain

7 From 2003 to 2006, the company was trying to achieve ....
   a) spectacular profits   b) steady growth   c) huge cost reductions

8 The company lost .... in 2007.
   a) $5.3bn   b) $3.5bn   c) $350m

9 Chapman Laney's situation improved after .... Roberts Ferguson.
   a) it was taken over by   b) it rejected a takeover bid by   c) it took over

10 Wurzel says that opportunities like the Roberts Ferguson takeover are ....
   a) unusual   b) common   c) rarely successful

SKILLS A **Match each of the functions (a–j) to the most appropriate phrase (11–20) below.**

11 At this stage, we want all your ideas, however crazy you think they are.

12 Could you give me some more details, please.

13 I was given your name by Albert Redding.

14 Are you saying you don't have that quantity in stock?

15 Let me give you an interesting statistic.

16 I don't think that would do us much good.

17 I really understand how you feel.

18 I'll have to get back to you on that one.

19 Would anyone like to ask any questions?

20 If you increase your order, we'll give you a bigger discount.

a) checking understanding   f) asking for feedback

b) expressing dissatisfaction   g) encouraging contributions

c) asking for further information   h) mentioning people you know

d) bargaining   i) exemplifying

e) playing for time   j) showing empathy

VOCABULARY **A** **Choose the best word to complete each sentence.**

21 Bev is an excellent salesperson because she's very (persuasive / reserved).

22 The (product / customer) profile is a description of the type of person who we expect to use the product.

23 The fire at our distribution centre (disrupted / soured) our ability to fill customer orders.

24 One reason that the (brand / workforce) is so successful may be its world-famous logo.

25 Bob didn't want to leave the job, but he was satisfied with the generous (severance payment / remuneration) when he finally had to go.

26 You can't eliminate risk but you can (negligibly / significantly) reduce it in most cases.

27 The employees really respect Adrian because he's supportive, inspiring, and (irresponsible / considerate).

28 We're having cashflow problems because some of our (debtors / creditors) haven't paid the money they owe us.

29 The most successful customer service teams give (payments / refunds) to customers who are dissatisfied and want to return a product.

30 Roberts Logistics and Global Postal and Telecom have set up a (joint venture / takeover) to run a new business parcel courier and delivery service in northern Europe.

READING **A** **Read the two articles on page 33. Match each heading (a–j) with the correct section in the articles.**

a) No to make-up, yes to moisturiser and shaving

b) Use an arrivals lounge

c) Plan your schedule

d) Pack efficiently

e) Take the right technology

f) Don't work on the plane

g) Wear the right clothes

h) Take time to readjust

i) Fly business, drink water

j) Keep fit

Business traveller: Long trips

A business trip of more than five days requires extra forethought and represents a bigger investment than a short stay. How do you ensure you don't come up short on your long trip?

.... 31

Think through the time assigned to the trip and what you hope to achieve. Get out your diary and plan. Alongside meetings that are fixed, you may find time to set up networking meetings – for instance, a lunch to get to know overseas colleagues and contacts better.

.... 32

How often do you use various items? What is essential? "Many people now choose not to take laptops," says Ms Robertson. "They find, if they are at a conference for a week, a smartphone combined with the hotel business centre is enough." Use technology to stay in touch with the office, but resist the urge to micromanage.

.... 33

Investigate your destination for lighter eating choices and exercise options. Activity to offset a rich restaurant-food diet need not require a gym – a 30-minute walk in a suitable local park is enough.

.... 34

The hardened business traveller doesn't take anything that does not fit in an overhead locker, says Ms Robertson. If you are having meetings with different people and are prepared to use hotel laundry services, your outfits can do double or triple duty. If you run out of shirts or socks, you can always buy more.

.... 35

Finally, on your return, try not to go straight from the airport to the office; take time to reflect on the trip and what you learnt.

FT FINANCIAL TIMES

Meetings after flights

For many executives, the most difficult meeting is the one you turn up to straight from a long-haul flight. What is the best way to ensure you are at your best?

.... 36

If ever there was a time to try to fly business, travelling with a meeting scheduled for when you arrive is it. A flat bed won't give you the best sleep ever, but you will sleep. Drink plenty of water but only a little alcohol and try to eat a light meal.

.... 37

Personal branding consultant Louise Mowbray advises against travelling in what you will wear to the meeting.

"At the very least, pack a fresh shirt and travel in a T-shirt. A fresh shirt makes a huge difference to how you feel in the morning," she says.

.... 38

Use the flight to relax – an extra hour of work is unlikely to transform a presentation, but an extra hour's sleep will change your mood. If you need to refresh your memory, print your notes to read in the cab on your way to the meeting.

.... 39

Women shouldn't put on cosmetics before they fly, as they will fall asleep in the dehydrating atmosphere of an aircraft with their make-up on. The combination is dreadful for your skin. Men should shave in the morning if possible, and both sexes should apply moisturiser.

.... 40

A number of airports offer arrivals lounges, including Lufthansa's Welcome lounge at Frankfurt, British Airways' arrivals lounge at Heathrow and Hong Kong's pay-in arrivals lounge. You can shower and freshen up, so it pays to investigate facilities at your destination before you start your journey.

FT FINANCIAL TIMES

A In the article, there is one mistake in each sentence. Identify the wrong word(s) and write the correct word(s) in the gaps (41–50) below.

VW stuns markets with €1bn jump in profits

Volkswagen surprises markets last Thursday by more than doubling its second-quarter operating profit.[41] The company also increased its cash reserves to a level described by one analyst as 'exception' high.[42]

The German multi-brand carmaker said its operating profit in the second quarter had gone above by more than €1bn to almost €2bn.[43] The increase was causing by a 20 percent jump in revenues to €61.8bn.[44]

The results were much better of analysts' forecasts.[45] Chief executive Martin Winterkorn said that first-half earnings was much higher than the company expected.[46]

The German carmaker will overtake its Japanese rival Toyota as the world's largest carmaker by 2018 if everything will go according to plan.[47] VW warned of a slowdown in growth in the second half of the year, but they are still very optimistic of profit.[48] VW's chief financial officer, Hans Dieter Pötsch, said that the company believes sell revenue and operating profit will be significantly higher than last year's figures.[49]

VW expects car sales rising partly because of strong growth in China.[50]

FINANCIAL TIMES

41 ....

42 ....

43 ....

44 ....

45 ....

46 ....

47 ....

48 ....

49 ....

50 ....

You work in the facilities management department of a small manufacturing firm. Your firm needs to purchase a new heating and cooling system for the warehouse. You have been asked to investigate three systems that would all be suitable from a technical point of view.

Use the data below and write a memo of 200–250 words to the purchasing manager. Tell him which system you would recommend and give your reasons.

	System A	System B	System C* (new system)
Purchase price (installation included)	€15,600	€19,500	€28,950
Annual running cost (based on energy use)	€4,100	€4,400	€2,900
Guarantee	1 year	3 years	5 years
Cost of service contract (after guarantee ends)	€850/year	€950/year	€950/year

SPEAKING

You are going to have a speaking test that will last about 15 minutes. There will be two parts:

Part A: You will be asked to prepare a short (3–4 minute) presentation.

Part B: You will have to ask for information about two companies, which you should then summarise and evaluate.

Part A: Presentation

Choose one of the topics below and prepare a short presentation. You should begin with a suitable introduction, divide the main information into about three main parts, and end with a conclusion. You can make notes but should not try to read the whole presentation. You will have about 15 minutes to prepare.

1 Make a presentation about an experience you have had with customer service. Explain the situation and describe the customer service. Explain what was good and what was bad and why. Describe how the customer service could be improved, or, if it was as good as it could be, explain how other companies could learn from your experience.

2 Make a presentation about a successful product. Give information about the product (what it is, who buys it, why it's so successful) and talk about the company (its size, nationality, main offices, etc.).

3 Make a presentation about a crisis that a company has had. What was the crisis? How did the company respond? How did the public perceive the response? Did the crisis ultimately help or hurt the company?

Part B: Gather information and summarising

You work for a company that produces mobile phones and laptop computers. Your company wants to take over a software company as a way to develop a 'package' that will include a laptop, a mobile phone and software that runs on both and makes them work well together. Ask the examiner for information about two possible companies: NuuSofft (based in Germany) and PDQriter (based in the US).

Try to get the following information about each company:

- type of software the company produces
- sales performance: how well they are selling
- when the company was set up
- market value
- profit last year
- share price trend

You can ask as many questions as you like to get the facts and check your understanding. You can make notes. When you have all the facts, you will be asked to make a summary comparing the two companies. You should then say which one you think offers the best potential for a takeover.

Audio scripts

The recordings of the material below can be found on the *Test Master CD-ROM*, which is at the back of the *Teacher's Resource Book*. Play each recording twice.

Entry test

🔊 2 (I = Isobel Reed, J = Joyce Payne)

I   Hi, Joyce. It's Isobel.

J   Oh, hello.

I   How's everything going?

J   Really well, thanks.

I   Good. I'm just in a taxi. I'm going to meet with the directors. Listen, I'm sorry to start your week with a problem, but I've just had a call from the Tokyo office, and they've just asked me to go over to Japan for an important meeting on Thursday. This means I'll be out of the office on Thursday and Friday, and we'll have to make some changes to the diary.

J   OK.

I   The first thing we need to change is the departmental meeting. We can't now hold this on Thursday morning, so I'd like to bring it forward to Wednesday afternoon at two o'clock.

J   OK.

I   Could you please e-mail everybody and check if that's OK?

J   Sure. I'll do that right away.

I   Thanks. Now, you know we've got to get the monthly report ready before that meeting.

J   Yes, right.

I   That means we need to finalise it by lunchtime on Wednesday at the latest. So could I schedule a meeting with you and Terry at ... let's say nine-thirty on Wednesday morning? It's just so we can go through the final details together. I'll have to cancel my lunch with Stephanie. But don't worry about that. I'll phone her this afternoon.

J   OK, fine.

I   The other urgent matter is the briefing meeting for the new management trainees on Friday. I'm afraid I won't be back in time for this. So perhaps we could re-arrange that meeting for next Monday? Can you let the trainees know as soon as possible about the change?

J   Sure, no problem. I'll take care of that today.

I   Great. Thanks. And those are the most urgent points. I'll have to reschedule the meeting with the legal department for next week. But that won't be a problem. And I expect there'll be some other arrangements to be changed as well but we can discuss those later. I'm in a meeting with the directors all morning and I won't be back at my desk until after lunch.

J   OK, good. See you then.

I   See you then. Bye!

J   Bye.

Progress test 1

🔊 **3** (L = Liz Parks, D = Darren Larson)

L How's it going in Southeast Asia, Darren?

D Things are going very well in Vietnam. It's definitely a growing market. Our sales are higher every quarter.

L That's good. What about Thailand?

D Sorry, I didn't quite catch that.

L I said what about Thailand?

D Well, I've seen last quarter's Thailand results and they're bad. They're really bad.

L What do you mean by really bad?

D They're about half of the previous quarter.

L Half?

D Yeah. It was the agent.

L Sorry, I'm not sure I know what you mean.

D Our agent in Thailand let us down.

L Could you explain that in more detail?

D Well, we thought we could count on him to book sales but he had no commitment, no motivation. In fact, we terminated his contract. We've already replaced him.

L ...

D Sorry, it's a terrible connection. Can I call you back?

L Sure. Bye!

D Bye!

L Hello?

D Hi, Darren.

L Ah, that's better. So ... when did the new agent start?

D He started last month.

L That's great news. Will he be at the regional conference in Singapore?

D Yes, he will. You can definitely meet him there.

L Good. Now, I want to tell you about my trip to ...

Progress test 2

🔊 **4** (S = Sara, A = Ahmed)

S You've been here for six months. How are you getting on, Ahmed?

A Well, honestly, the first few weeks I really wondered if I'd made the right decision taking the job.

S Really? Tell me about that.

A Well, at first I liked the important job title – sales manager – but I never had any time off. I had to work all the time – including weekends – to get the job done.

S Yes, we noticed that. But it got better, didn't it?

A That's right. I have very supporting colleagues and a hard-working boss ...

S Heh, heh ...

A ... well, it's true ... and now I really, really enjoy coming to work.

S OK, you put in the hard work to learn the job, what keeps you interested in it now?

A Well, I'm in sales, right, and like a lot of sales managers, my main motivation is the financial incentive. Being in sales means that I can increase my salary because of my efforts – the more my team sell, the more I can earn.

S And we've all seen the result of your efforts, Ahmed. Like you, we were worried at first. But we know you're the right man for the job because the sales figures tell us that. Do you have any concerns? Is anything bothering you?

A The only thing that worries me right now is the global economy. Business for us is good but everything's a bit unstable at the moment – I don't think anyone's really safe.

S You're right about that but of course ...

🔊 **5** (S = Sara, H = Howard)

S Howard, you've been doing well enough, but you seem a little low on energy. Is everything OK?

H I guess I'm feeling like a small part of a very big machine.

S Tell me more about that.

H Working in HR, I like the contact with people and I like the problem-solving but someone saying 'well done' now and again would be nice. When sales are up, the sales team have a party and no one remembers or thinks about my contribution.

S I have to say that I see what you mean. It's the nature of the job you do. But I wonder if we could find a way to make it more satisfying for you.

H OK ...

S You're not going to get the same glory that the sales team get but what do you really value? What could we change to make life better?

H Funny you should ask that, Sara. I've been thinking that I'd like to work from home some of the time, maybe a day a week, but the way meetings are scheduled, I think it would be tough. And I think the company is keen on people being in the office.

S Well, that's been true in the past, certainly, but basically we like your work, Howard. You're a valuable member of the team and we want to keep you feeling fresh and energised.

H The main thing for me is flexibility and I guess freedom ...

Progress test 3

 6

Hello, and welcome. My name's Lydia Jones. I'm in charge of training at A–Z Airlines. I'm very happy that all of you have joined our team.

The purpose of my talk today is to explain A–Z Airlines' approach to teambuilding. I hope by the end of my presentation, you'll understand the importance of teamwork on the job.

As I'm sure you're all aware, one of the most important professional skills cabin crew have is the ability to work as a team.

There are four key elements to teamwork: leadership, knowledge and skills, working systems, and relationships.

First, leadership. Every team needs a leader. Especially when things are happening quickly, someone needs to be decisive and to organise work efficiently. This doesn't mean the leader is ruthless or authoritarian. A good leader is also a good listener, motivator, mediator and friend.

Moving on to the second element of teamwork ... this is what you bring to work with you every day: your knowledge and skills. You've all been hired to work at A–Z Airlines because you've shown that you already have some of the knowledge and skills that you'll need for the job. As you continue your training and all through your career, you'll continue to gain knowledge and skills that'll make you a better team member every time you come to work.

OK, now I'll talk about working systems. You could describe working systems as rules, but they aren't rules that stop you doing something, they're rules that allow you to work efficiently. Working in an airplane, we do certain jobs the same way every time. This means that everyone knows exactly how the job is done, and it also means that we're doing the job in the safest possible way.

Right, now turning to relationships. What does this mean? Well, teamwork in a way is all about relationships. What we all have to remember is that the team is there to do a job safely and efficiently. Everyone is trying their best. Sometimes people make mistakes. What we have to remember is that the job of the team is what we have to concentrate on. It's important to think about what you're doing but you also have to think about what the entire team is doing and you have to have constant, open communication with your team-mates. So that's what we mean by *relationships*.

OK, does anyone have any questions so far?

Progress test 4

🔊 7 (M = Martin, S = Susan)

M Customer service. How can I help?

S Oh, hello. Er ... I'm having a problem with my phone.

M Oh, I'm sorry to hear that. What's the problem?

S I've just switched over to your company. Your engineer has just left.

M Our engineer has just visited your house?

S Yes, that's right.

M And what happened?

S Well, I have two phones in my house. One upstairs, one downstairs.

M OK ...

S And this morning, before your engineer arrived to change me over to your service, both phones worked fine.

M OK ...

S And now, the upstairs phone doesn't work at all. The downstairs phone is fine, but the upstairs one is dead.

M Did you tell the engineer about the problem?

S Well, after he finished his work, I went upstairs to make sure the phone was working. When I came back downstairs, the engineer was already outside in his van. He was in a real rush. He was very rude!

M So what did you do next?

S I ran outside and told him that he couldn't go - the upstairs phone didn't work. He broke my phone!

M Are you saying that he left without repairing your phone?

S Yes, that's right. He said he had to get to his next job, and that I'd have to phone you to set up another repair visit. I feel really upset about that.

M I'm not surprised you're upset.

S I need that upstairs phone! My office is upstairs, and I need the phone for work!

M OK, so what you're saying is that you asked the engineer to come back inside and check the problem, but he refused?

S Yes, that's exactly right.

M OK, listen. I'm going to take some information from you, and we're going to get someone out to look at your phone later today, if you'll be at home.

S Yes, I'll be at home.

M OK, could you please confirm that your address is ...

Exit test

🔊 **8** (I = Interviewer, V = Vic)

I   You came to Chapman Laney in the middle of a crisis. A lot of people thought the company was going to go under. What was wrong with Chapman Laney?

V   Chapman Laney had lost its way. For almost 60 years, we'd been a corporate advisor. Then the management started wanting to be like Goldman Sachs – a huge investment bank.

I   In what way?

V   The company started taking big risks on the stock market and in the property and private equity markets.

I   So did you make a lot of changes as soon as you arrived?

V   I did. We immediately stopped risking so much company money on big, high-risk deals. I brought in about 500 new traders. They buy and sell securities for our clients. That's what the business originally did, when it started back in 1954. We're investing in retail again, not hedge funds. We need to get away from the high-risk investment world and back to a more stable business model.

I   So how do you measure the success of the business?

V   Well, in the early two thousands – 2003 to 2006, say – we were looking for a really big performance every quarter. All I cared about then was profit. Things have changed. Now I want to see something steady – steady progress, not huge profits.

I   What happened in 2007?

V   That was a bad year. The company took a 3.5 billion dollar loss on the sub-prime mortgage trade. We almost lost everything. It took us three years to get out of that. Then a big turning point came when we had a chance to take over Roberts Ferguson, the retail brokerage. Some people thought that deal was very risky but in that case, I think I really did know what I was doing.

I   That was a big part of getting Chapman Laney back in the black, wasn't it?

V   Absolutely right. It was a once-in-a-lifetime opportunity. And we made it work.

Guidelines for the examiner

Examiner's notes: Speaking tests

It is recommended that the oral test be recorded on tape for analysis afterwards. Oral performance should always be assessed by at least two teachers. In the event of disagreement, award a score midway between the two (if two assessors), or take an average (if three or more assessors).

The oral performance of candidates with a pass score of 8 or more can be described as follows: *The candidate can use English to communicate effectively and consistently, with few hesitations or uncertainties.*

Description based on level 7 of the English speaking Union's Framework of Examination Levels.

Entry Test: Speaking

This test should take 10 minutes per candidate. Candidates each give a 5 minute presentation and then answer your questions about it.

Allow candidates time to prepare. While one candidate is being tested, the next one can prepare their presentation.

Notes on assessment:

Total 15 marks. Award 3 marks each for:
- Fluency and confidence
- Overall comprehensibility (including clear pronunciation)
- Accuracy and appropriacy of language
- Ability to organise ideas and structure the presentation
- Range of language (grammar, function phrases, vocabulary)

Exit Test: Speaking

This test should take about 15 minutes per candidate. There are two parts:

- Part A: a short (3–4 minute) presentation
- Part B: gathering information about two companies, making a summary, and stating (with reasons) which one offers the best potential for a takeover

While one candidate is being tested, the next one can prepare their presentation.

The information you need to give the candidate in Part B is set out in the boxes below. This is a test of the candidate's ability to ask questions. Do not volunteer information unless asked specifically for it.

NuuSofft	PDQriter
Produces apps popular with Apple iPhone users.	Produces database software.
Sales: Excellent. Produced a best-selling app (DataXlinx) which has sold over 2 million downloads.	Sales: steady, not spectacular. But the company has recently released a piece of software that is being described by reviewers as 'revolutionary'.
The company was set up 6 years ago.	The company was set up only 2 years ago.
Market value: €350 million	Market value: €176 million
Profit last year: €71 million	Profit last year: €29 million
Share price: Has been increasing over the last year and currently stands at €1.02.	Share price: Has remained at about €0.71 since the company went public last year.

Notes on assessment

Part A: Presentation. Total 5 marks. Award 1 mark each for:
- Fluency and confidence
- Overall comprehensibility
- Accuracy and appropriacy of language
- Ability to organise ideas and structure the presentation
- Range of language (grammar, functional phrases, vocabulary)

Part B: Gathering information. Total 10 marks.

Award 4 marks for:
- Good questioning and ability to get all the facts by asking for repetition or clarification where necessary

Award 2 marks each for:
- Inclusion of all facts in the summary
- Ability to organise ideas and give reasons for choice
- Accuracy and appropriacy of language

Examiner's notes: Writing tests

For each writing task award a maximum of 15 marks, 3 for each of these criteria:
- Including all the information required
- Politeness (thanking, looking forward to meeting, etc.)
- Organisation and clear structuring of ideas
- Accuracy of language (grammar, functional phrases, vocabulary, etc.)
- Range of language (grammar, functional phrases, vocabulary, etc.)

Pearson Education Limited
Edinburgh Gate
Harlow
Essex CM20 2JE
England
and Associated Companies throughout the world.

www.pearsonlongman.com
© Pearson Education Limited 2011

First published 2011
Tenth impression 2019

ISBN 978 1 4082 1999 7

Set in Metaplus 9.5/12.5pt
Printed by Ashford Colour Press Ltd

Acknowledgements

We are grateful to the following for permission to reproduce copyright material:

Text

Extract from "Ask the experts: Be clear what you stand for", *The Financial Times*, 04/06/2010 (quotation by Rita Clifton, UK Chairman of Interbrand), reproduced with permission of Interbrand; Extract from "Ask the experts: Be clear what you stand for", *The Financial Times*, 04/06/2010 (quotation by David Molian, Director of the Business Growth and Development Programme at Cranfield School of Management), reproduced with permission of Cranfield School of Management; Extract from "Ask the experts: Ask questions and listen to answers", *The Financial Times*, 29/01/2010 (Moules, J.), (quotation by Mark Savinson, Accredit Ltd), reproduced with permission of Accredit Ltd; Extract adapted from "Business traveller: Long trips", *The Financial Times*, 04/05/2010 (Rigby, R.), copyright © Rhymer Rigby; and Extract adapted from "Meetings after flights", *The Financial Times*, 20/04/2010 (Rigby, R.), copyright © Rhymer Rigby.

The Financial Times

Extract adapted from "Trendspotter: Capsule hotels", *The Financial Times*, 01/05/2010 (Vaisey, H.), copyright © The Financial Times Ltd; Extract from "Japanese companies seek local leaders abroad", *The Financial Times*, 29/06/2010 (Soble, J.), copyright © The Financial Times Ltd; Extract adapted from "Social networking: Schools struggle to balance openness with control", *The Financial Times*, 15/03/2010 (Bradshaw, T.), copyright © The Financial Times Ltd; Extract from "Venture capital hit by 'slump' in funding", *The Financial Times*, 07/07/2010 (Guthrie, J.), copyright © The Financial Times Ltd; and Extract from "Learning from crime", *The Financial Times*, 11/07/2010 (Eddy, K.), copyright © The Financial Times Ltd.

In some instances we have been unable to trace the owners of copyright material, and we would appreciate any information that would enable us to do so.

Front cover image: Fotolia: SuzyM
Project managed by Chris Hartley